Flying Fish

ANTONY DUNN was born in London in 1973. He won the 1995 Newdigate Prize while reading English at St Catherine's College, Oxford. His first collection of poems, *Pilots and Navigators*, was published by Oxford in 1998, and he received an Eric Gregory Award in 2000. He also writes for film and the stage, and lives in York, where he works as Marketing Manager for Riding Lights Theatre Company and Friargate Theatre.

Also by Antony Dunn from OxfordPoets

Pilots and Navigators

ANTONY DUNN

Flying Fish

Oxford*Poets*

CARCANET

First published in Great Britain in 2002 by
Carcanet Press Limited
4th Floor, Conavon Court
12–16 Blackfriars Street
Manchester M3 5BQ

A CIP catalogue record for this book
is available from the British Library

ISBN 1 903039 56 8

The publisher acknowledges financial assistance
from the Arts Council of England

Set in Monotype Bembo by XL Publishing Services, Tiverton
Printed and bound in England by SRP Ltd, Exeter

                                    catch
   the otherlife of things
                              before a look
  immerses them.

      John Burnside
      from 'Fields', *The Asylum Dance*

Acknowledgements

Acknowledgements are due to the following publications: *Artyfact*, *A Clatter of Choughs* (ed. Lucy Newlyn), *Dreamcatcher*, *Envoi*, *Forward Book of Poetry* 1999, *The Frogmore Papers*, *The Independent*, *The New Writer*, *The Observer*, *The Oxford Magazine*, *Oxford Poetry*, *Poetry London*, *Point Shirley*, *Quadrant*, *The Reater*, *Thumbscrew*.

'Bombing a Publisher' was especially written for *A Commonplace Book (Carcanet 1970–2000)* to celebrate Carcanet's thirtieth year.

'Waxy Bembo' makes reference to two poems by Norman MacCaig, 'Hugh MacDiarmid' and 'Cliff Top, East Coast'.

And thanks to Jacky Flurscheim, Siân Williams and Matthew Hollis; and to the Society of Authors for an Eric Gregory Award in 2000 and for their sponsorship of the *First Lines* Poetry Tour 2001, for which thanks are also due to the Arts Council of England and the Camden Trust.

Contents

Flying Fish

Stretched out and painted a clownish blue
it is the ugliest souvenir
in the airport gift-shop.

What we take home is the filigree
of sparks and splashes around our boat
late in the night-time cruise.

Not this keepsake of scales and fin-bones,
of toy-blind eyes, rheumy and varnished,
wings bleached dry as moth-dust,

but the blur of the dazzled moment
when you missed the single flying fish
I thought I might have seen.

Arcing out from our catamaran,
it was fluid, quicker than my tongue
splayed in its stiff-hinged case.

Some question unsilvered in my throat,
or something not pointed out in time,
slabbed by salt, heat, the turn of your back
at that precise instant.

Explosives

Scuppered by the guns in Bridgetown harbour
when fire on board conspired with its cargo,
the ship is alive, eighty years later.
The hold pulses with its unstable load
of fish, wary near the polyp'd cases,
whose unlikely colours are fugitive
from the warm tank of the television.

Your snorkel discharges its buoyant shot
as you sink into the hull – bikini'd
frogwoman in this element's flippers –
through the field of impassive jellyfish
primed to detonate against skin. Then this
ticking in my chest as you rise past me
to the boat's ladder, and climb out backwards.

Low Tide

A mile from the dead harbour we step up
to a wide silt beach, its thin river
filling with the merge of Wales and England.
No landmarks between the two horizons
except one troubled sail of smoke, leaning
from the keel-toppled disarray of boats.

The clothes-iron scorch of a vaporised hull
shimmers the air to a watery haze
across forgotten creases of the dunes,
and the reek of machine oil and woodsmoke
is like the bonfire night when we held hands
in your coat pockets, spooned close to the flames.

We melt the soles of our shoes balancing
on the ash-glowing rails, and rechristen
our boat with a swung salute of spit which
mousses and fizzes into heady air.
The grassy sand liquefies around us,
the skyline gathers up its plunge and heave;

and we figurehead the sea-facing prow,
your shoulder blades buoyant against my chest.
What I mean by whatever I whisper
into your ear is that I steer by you;
that you'll take me back to this casting-off
when I smell smoke in your hair years from now.

Bathing

When you hung in holiday blue
in that white–blue water
which made of your body something
I could almost pass my hand through,
like water, I may have guessed

how you would stand in honeymoon red,
fixed in amber bath-light,
and make of your body something
bold as a tap's flex of water.
Or how you would make me think

that even one quick molecule
of that courting sea might,
by sun, by rain, have crossed from there
to here, to make of your body
something in its element.

Radio

What sounds like the broadcast of snow itself
among mountains visible only by
the absence of stars, is the radio's
wheezing stagger between its lost stations.

Half an hour of the sky's current affairs
murmur in the back of the car
as we order orange digits this way
and that in the dashboard's familiar dark;

until a voice stags the black—white airwaves.
She announces herself like the smell of
cocoa, or of grandparents' bed-linen,
turns the radio's display to a hearth.

Aunty Jean, anachronist in-between
the songs of her Sunday night music-show,
talks us through unguessable lochs and drops
of this road through the Highlands, and the snow

mothing our headlights. Outside this warm space
untold deer, in their camouflage, adjust
their antennae to the white-noised engine,
deaf to the one broadcast passing through them.

She's not really called Aunty Jean, she says,
as the radio loses her,
and the dark air empties itself again
of everything but darkness and the snow.

Dolphins

A beach which makes sense of shipping forecasts;
a light-housed spit just shy of Cromarty.
We came here along the edge of Loch Ness,
pretending our search through the Super 8
flicker of January trees was jest.

In the honeymoon hire-car the wipers
and our breath on the glass conspire against
binoculars, and we are forced out,
waterproofs cracking and flapping like sails,
onto the muscular whim of pebbles.

A small hundred dolphins in these waters –
and we are obstinate at the tide's hem,
the backs of our jeans clinging to shivers,
the fictions of waves making up monsters
for half an hour, fifty minutes, an hour.

Then you stamp with impatience – such a drive,
such cold – and there one is. Definite, black.
And another. And there, and there, and there.
Five or six, not far out, leaping as if
they were the very joy of something born,

something embarked upon. And all language,
all experience, is reduced to *there*;
that sparse abundance making an Eden
of this desolate place, making of us
more than wet spectators on a wet beach.

Elgol

The first thing is the hurrying away
from the car's exhaust fumes; the parking space
guilty as the rock where the last Great Auk
coughed up its selfless final vital signs;

then the comic shock of sheep where slipway
hesitates into stones and becomes beach.
We stumble after their foot-rattling flight
along the ocean's uncertain border,

treading carefully as if each pebble
were an egg which might split and spill fossils
from which we'd recognise ourselves evolved.
The sheep are gone beyond the one wrecked house.

The frontier air is heavy with water
where we can half-feel gills opening up
beneath breathable fabrics of collars,
fingers gathering numb cold like scaled mittens.

The last thing is the sea's urging us home;
leave your small senses folded on the beach —
there is only one way away from here
if not the hard road up into hard mountains.

Extraction

Skull fathomer,
spotlighting submariner,
the x-ray sweeps into its eye
a moment of bones
white as the scrawling crabs,
blind and bleached by depth,
morsing the thoughts of oceans.

Trace on the film
the indistinct curve, itching
to burst from its bed, of one last
wisdom tooth, its wince
the braille of cell-divide;
read in its root-rings
the sinking back of Plesiosaurs

into their own blueprint –
one sparking synapse
in the mind of God.

Cœlacanth

It should have been dead these millions of years.
A couple off the Cape – hardly enough
to call a shoal – and they thought that was it.

Now some South Sea island you'd have been hard pushed
to name: a fisherman charades the corpse
through the warm shallows which finished it off.

Unconvincing as a leather model
of itself, it's an ugly specimen,
nearly chucked for having bad, oily meat.

And the European scientist who
found it at a rock-bottom price
on a stall of sleek, silvery bodies

explains to the camera how there's no way
to tell its age and how, for all he knows,
we could be looking at millennia.

Evolution turned a blind eye. The fish
kept itself to itself, then gave in to
a technology of bent wire and string.

As its hollow spine yields to pressureless
air, warming in eight-minute-old sunlight,
a strange language of bubbles at its mouth

blabs the first of its secrets – of feeding
mating, migration – robs us of something.
Marvel at its miracle ugliness.

Rejoice that scientists and fishermen
are still landing evidence that there might be
some thing, one thing, we know nothing about.

Balloon Pilot in Church

You wouldn't have known it, but we had met
already through the television news.
That Sunday when, in undoubtable flesh,
you stood up front with your harmonica
and breathed out your strange vocabulary,
you were the living proof of something else;

as if you were trying to explain how
the silken globe had blossomed around you
in a hot riot of petals, as if
it were the entire weight of Pentecost
covering you with a quick liquid tongue;
and how you could remember none of it.

One note, as taut as power cables or
the blue-lined grief of bedside instruments,
jolts my heart off course; a cold-dropped balloon.
Neither air nor fire is our element,
nor is this rapid up-rush of true earth
anywhere truthfully to call our own.

Wrestling with Angels

The way he tapped wafers of cuttlefish
with propitiatory fingers
into the backyard aviary
was the way he cleaned the stained glass windows;
his focus falling far beyond
the budgerigar colours. So.

Perhaps some annunciation of light
quickening the still life of glass
surprised him like fox-fluttered wings,
but his wife was looking the other way
and he can't recall. The neighbours
are calling it a miracle:

how he hammered his palms against the lead
and balanced his ladder upright
for a moment – then the slow curve.
Transfigured, arms ablaze with coloured plumes,
he wrestled a night-long angel
down the up-rushing rungs of light.

But his wife did see how he came to rest –
his arms spread across the altar,
his gaze rolling the roof away –
how he stood up, walked with his hip knocked out
and came home the same man, the world
flapping and squawking around him.

In the backyard he drops seeds through the bars,
stares through the golds and greens of birds.
Doesn't like to talk about it.
And he wears the colours of his one bruise
lightly, as if they were nothing
but a buffet from a bright wing.

This Morning

1 January 2000

From where I'm standing it's blindingly clear.
The sun, like Sisyphus, trembles with strain

to heave the boiling boulder of itself
up the summitless slope of horizons.

Slow as a colt through a crowd, it's baffled,
shoulders its punishment and shrugs us off;

our six billion voices cheering *welcome*,
thundering like palm leaves onto its path.

Breakfast on the Beach

Early sun twists slights of mist from the skin
of the sea, and the air itches
with gathering heat.

Through the charcoal's smoke and shimmer, above
the stick-skewered silvers of fish,
we hardly knew him.

As we beach the heavy boat, the thin scent
of costly oils lifts from him through
smells of wood and flesh

and this we remember well from the day
we stood beneath him and downwind
on a bleak hillside.

The sun, winding itself up to break free
from the water's dark meniscus,
treads the sea lightly

as the waves make their nervous approaches,
hushing and stammering, surprised,
shy as mourning friends.

Glory

The swing of Bridget's front gate
disturbs the marigold-head
of bright yellow spider eggs
suspended mid-frame.

A scirr of invisible
legs, and a dozen tiny
bodies quicken on the web's
improbable spokes,

new-hatched to the idea
of gravity, or learning
the mob's decoy centrifuge;
its precise panic.

In the annunciation
of this late-spring sunset's breeze
we believe that these hundreds
of spiders might spin

their angel-sails and, with two
front legs delicate as faith,
leave go of their globe and lift
like pollen or ash.

With knowledge of birds tasting
like a penny on the tongue
we covet this letting go,
this unencumbrance.

Snow Storm

At the skip-end of York Minster
five fathoms up, a carved prow
breaks from the tempestuous stone –

a miracle of settled snow
on the storm-placating arms
of Christ, his crew's fear-frozen heads.

This great up-rearing wave refutes
the blizzard, holds up the life
of stones to the enduring sky.

Lindisfarne

Across the causeway
  a traffic of fish
    shivers out of sight;
moon cobbles water
  miraculously
    from the imagined shore
to the jetty's six,
  seven, six steps down
    onto the hard sea.
Behind us, a school
  of spine-arching hulls
    heaves from rolling grass
and ahead the road,
  the light like blindness,
    two steps to the water
to test our small faith
  for boldness enough
    to belong where we land.

Swim

Exuberant green mousses the prow
under a sail bursting with sky,
and the edge of the flat earth happens
beneath a keel which, in an instant,
is immeasurably high
in black water.

Heart and lungs cold-clamped by the dive,
the crawl away from the boat fails
to rub life into skin or quicken
sluggish blood. Current-carried, too far,
quick gasps frightening themselves
in mist-thick air,

this buoying head is the centre
of a perfect globe of distances;
a world of water, one element
whose single muscle is too taut
to flex into feature. Hung
in empty space,

this ear tunes to some inaudible
siren, and the eye must look down.
The black weight of everything crowds
against the few square inches of mask.
The heart gapes like a black hole;
in shrinking lungs

air clings to itself and its holt
like the last gasp of a species.
Amid teeming, dread imaginings,
this pale planet of restless limbs
is the hub of gravity
in the blackness.

The swim-wake is heavy as panic,
heel-dragging a guessed course through mist
towards the boat's unsteady comforts
of brass and wood, canvas and rope,
its edge slippy as nightmares.
In its own place,

it is the sudden shark which calms;
calm as a hull keeling air-fathoms
in its one, indifferent direction,
certain that everything revolves
round the gravity gaping
in its black gut.

Salt Water

Yellow as a joke,
the squat submarine
crunches through surface-
water for a grip
to drag itself down.

Lead-bellied, glass-nosed,
it hauls slowly down
a straight rope of light
through thickening dark
to the sudden bed.

Light sweeps like radar
through the salt-tripled
weight of the Dead Sea
across a surface
blanker than the moon.

Disputed waters:
nudging a border
which bisects the site
(photo'd from space) of
a city-shadow,

our pilot ignites
a Political
Incident, stirring
contour-circles round
square miles of nothing.

Staring at this depth
along the searchlight,
his eyeballs throb, clogged
with the ice-glitter
of flat miles of salt.

The tinny voice from
fathoms above sends
his heart belly-up;
I'm gonna have to
bring you up now.

Searchlight skating like
a blind man's finger
on a printed page,
the sub lights up;
turquoise, cyan, white.

The salt hands it back,
yellow as a joke,
to the air buzzing
with questions which will
have to be answered.

Robinson Joins the Navy

'to see the world' — Robinson

Hydraulics like the muscles of the sea
buoy the three decks of mocked-up battleship.
Half a mile from the ocean, the sun skims
a desert-smell from the doldrum tarmac,
heat simulating water, ankle-deep.

Matelot Robinson shoulders his satchel
of spruce wedges, fidgets his thumb around
the absence of his mallet's safety catch
sticks his boot into the first rung and up
to his below-the-water-line station.

Somewhere in the machine, someone presses
a button and Robinson, the wrong side
of the observation glass, finds sea-legs
as the pistons make-believe their fathoms,
his bowels lurching like a half-mile of hose

filling with salt water, invisibly
quick as shells. He is memorising each
puncture-wound's breath-taking maw, waiting for
the moment's darkness before red half-light,
his mallet flimsy as a sling in his

small grasp, his faith slip-smooth as wet pebbles.
Blood rehearses rhythms in his ear's hull —
the hammer-stride of ocean shaking steel
like tent-hide; its giant roar, its language
like an echo of ancestry; *now kill*

or be killed, sailor, or abandon ship.

Goldfish

Of course, it all began at the fairground
with the plastic bag and its single fish
like a magic sweet.

That, and the colour of the water-light
in the darkness of the aquarium
at Regent's Park zoo.

★

How the dappling blue from the bedroom tank
lay along the body of his young wife,
jewelling down and sheen;

and how the fish gaped at their liquid sprawl
mouthing *o, o, o,* and fluttering fins
coy as paper fans.

★

How aquaria scaled the living room;
tank after tank, big as pyramid blocks
with their quick treasure,

up the four walls, on shelves above the door,
the TV viewed through a lens of water
and blundering fish.

How he lip-read her complaints – *o, o, o* –
deaf as glass in the water-light, when he
took out the light-bulb

and took to sleeping in his chair, among
the Commons, the Bubble-Eyes and Fantails,
the Celestials.

How the air was spiced with weed, and sluggish
with the weight of water. Sealed – him, never
coming out, nor her in.

★

The suitcase down the stairs, the slammed front door,
shake the gold blizzard of his toy-storm room
which never settles.

Still in its midst, the bang sets him thinking.
Clear out the basement, the dust-fossils of
wedding gifts, memories;

waterproof the walls, run a hosepipe in.
Lay a new glass floor in the living room,
buy a modest shark.

And the goldfish, quietly clamouring,
stare in at him as a sleepy thought sparks
in the bowl of his skull;

a whole town of roof-top salt-water tanks,
and the blue sky alive with flying fish,
skimming home after home.

Vanilla

Flavour of no flavour at all,
we thought, brought up on cheap ice cream
in a village where the mothers
and wives use a secret language.

One pod, black as crape, at the bed
of a jar of foam-white sugar,
lid snug as a submarine hatch,
left on a sea-ward window sill

for the duration. It sweetens
with sympathy their endless tea:
their common tongue, unpetalling
like cream-coloured flowers on tongues

stiff and cold as stones. How they stand
among flotsam – sift the air for
one scent scrambling from the surf – or,
with faces pale as unlit lamps

at the salt-flawed windows of home,
watch for tall clouds coming like sails
of one colour or another
from the far edge of the ocean.

Connecticut

i.m. Pamela Dunn

I never saw New England in the fall,
but they say that the trees which make it so
perfect for movies are gold as awards
in the low-slung flattering of late sun.

My camera memory fixes you here;
edits the accidental shadows
of its cherry-picker hoist flicking
through leaves like a fish-fiction among stones,

frames you square among these bright paradigms,
these miles of tarnishings – rust leaves, breeze-mobbed,
applauding like a million loosed reel-ends.

A to Z

Whether or not the balding cockatoo
survived her, no one has thought to mention.
So now she is in a coffin somewhere;
her husband a doll in an outsized house,
absurd as a new pupil fidgeting
in first-term blazer and grow-into shoes.

And now his taxi is not the refuge
it was the last time I almost saw him –
too much room in the back of the black car –
and he's turning, red-eyed, in the cage
of his front room, through film of net curtains
and oiled antimacassars. He fits his feet

to the barenesses of stair-carpet, prints
his body into the wide, restless bed.
He asks his sister-in-law for his girl's
address; writes that her mother asked for her.
Has to look in a road atlas to find
the town. Didn't know that was her surname.

The man who never used an A to Z
in the last forty years doesn't know if
he's coming or going. I imagine
all this, for want of actual knowledge;
picture him at home in Chiswick, Chelsea,
Battersea, Lambeth, Southwark, Greenwich.

Homebrew

for my father

A keepsake, the tang of your homebrewed beer
which is a dozen scents:

the autumny rustle of hops in one
leg of tied-off nylons,

dust in the carved back of the bishop's throne
on which the barrel stood,

watery reminiscences at mouths
of rinsed, waiting bottles,

the giant's breath of the forbidden peek
into the yeasty dark.

Then that first bewildering sip of it,
the bitterness where taste

meets smell; how you said I'd grow to like it.
Your shirts are part of it,

and the sour ink in the study's hand-cranked
duplicating machine.

The wanting to give you back your sense of
smell, smashed out in a cab.

Your gifts are hoardings – months of Arts pages
from the Sunday papers

or a bag of conkers on the doorstep.
I am collecting you

piece by piece. Or rather, fermenting you
from guessed ingredients.

Seafood Suite

i. Mussels

for Janis

You arrive as we're finishing the job –
gaping purple shells clucking, open-mouthed,

into one bowl, and another brimming
with the too tight-lipped in their rock-pool scum.

Six of us cling to the kitchen table
which has mutely witnessed such unshellings.

A slip of the tongue undoes each secret
creature, slithering warmly from its berth.

Not for me, you say, surprising yourself
by crying over your surprise entrée.

ii. Octopus

for my mother

Corridors of peep-show neon – green, blue –
the skin-crawling skins of deep-sea creatures,

bored nakedness of rays, sea-lions' act,
and the harsh lesson of the octopus:

detention in a glass-topped prep-school desk.
Androgynous sac, flexing with instinct,

filling her dunce's corner with dumb waves;
the eight-handed caress of fresh water,

the weakening stroke through no roof-hung eggs,
the hunger unshaping her restless frame.

iii. Prawns

for Robyn

These warm shapes, slippy as a fist of sea
in your fish-out-of-water unfocus,

mean *mother*. Your first night home she eats prawns,
breaking at last her eight-month seafood fast;

the fierce snap of tail and head, the easing
of naked curls from their papery shells,

the hunger to do with octopus love.
And you, big-bummed aphid in your lime-green,

gape at the nipple's miraculous sap,
marvel – water to wine; milk and honey.

Cardboard Box

i.m. Denise Goss

It comes bobbing in, folded together
neat as a newspaper boat; leaves the aisle
like a wake, disturbing the flat we tread.

Out like a paper aeroplane, scorching
shrouds of air, indelibly gone, shouldered
by the four men it takes to hold you down.

And down like an envelope you've opened
and emptied and dropped behind you, the news
all good.

Afterwards

White blossom breaks from the cherry tree's snow.
The opulent branches are over-spent;
everything turning to water. We go

through the conservatory, sun-filled below
the bay tree, whose leaves we snap for their scent.
White blossom breaks from the cherry tree's snow.

Along the path through fat sunlight we're slow,
the creaked-in prints of soles quick to relent –
everything turning to water. We go

down to the lawn, skin hot with cold – aglow –
make angels on our backs. Nothing is meant.
White blossom breaks from the cherry tree's snow,

and the wide-eyed, eye-blue sky weeps as though
the sun, rolling itself aside, has sent
everything turning to water. We go

back into your house – not the house you'd know.
Easter is stirring in its shroud of Lent.
White blossom breaks from the cherry tree's snow,
everything turning to water. We go.

One

Where the cliff-top path has lost its footing
and thrown itself into the abandon,
I am fulmar-winged with love, vertigo
mewing over its tapping egg, this heart.

Perched on a post, the camera is gaping
to grasp all the blues of two elements
whose divide is lost in unfocused mist.

The quick self-timer catches me flying,
blurring into you. One step from the edge,
your catching me might be your upswing catch
at the root of the wing of a white horse,

our arms motion-feathered like a sentence
of metamorphosis – lovers, centaured,
treading unfathomable blue distance.

Glider

In the time it takes to climb
                two thousand feet
before the aerotow comes loose
                and we bank left
away from the tow-plane's guide
                there is much to learn
about instinct –

                the equivocal dials
of the inner ear
                the alignment
of horizon and nose-cone
                being more or less true
than the accuracy
                of busy instruments

about the magnet
                in the skull of a goose
insubstantial as the idea
                of home
and the tilt of the wing
                toward the field
where you are waiting

                to drive us back
through miles made strange with mist
                and altitude
to the house where we are woken
                morning after morning
by the certainty of geese
                pointing *home* above our bed>

Rising

And darling, the way you leapt from the bed
with what seemed, just then, like unseemly haste,
threw open the fridge, the kitchen cupboards
and banged a slapdash mix into a bowl
and worked up a warm dough and kneaded it,
naked and streaked with flour at the worktop,
was enough.
          How you bent to the oven,
flushed in its bold breath, slid in the pale loaf
and straightened, wreathed in the perfume of yeast.
How the house filled with the ill-kept secret
of rising as you set the timer, turned
to come back at me with your floury hands.

No Bridge

York Millennium Bridge delayed – December 1999

Ducks jam the waterway, honking
  like armoured cars along a wall
    between one state and another,
  the banks' ferry-scars grown over.

Strange as doppelgängers, walking
  to work, or to opposite shops
    for milk and English newspapers,
  we are at home, visa-distant,

a reflected kilometre
  from the first crossing between us.
    And yet the east bank's effluent
  is much like the shit from the west.

And when the lights go out along
  Hospital Fields Road, when the cats
    are put out on Butcher Terrace,
  our attics do not fill with dreams

of the day when a gang with picks
  and democratic sledge-hammers
    will smash the river's stony scorn
  with a whoop of concrete and steel.

While these rumpled banks are still green,
  where geese pillow undisturbed heads
    in warm linen of limbs, this is
  a grass too steep for walking on.

Persephone in the Exclusion Zone

A time of fires
and the men shaving their heads
outdoors with shearing clippers
or standing around the fires
kicking the embers' edges
with hard-nosed boots.

The low chorus
is cattle-song at the mouth
of the tear of the top-soil,
shadowing my uphill path
with all the anguish of love
gone underground.

Seven light steps
beyond the road block, the grass
at my feet freshens with sparks,
smokes wraiths of pomegranate –
daffodils, hot-tongued, leaping
to cleanse us of this.

Breaking News

And thinking of *Breakfast at Tiffany's*,
this was something you'd never done; weighing
news like a too-expensive ring.

And it came in, smart as a gift-wrapped box,
with a thud like your hands on the bonnet
of a crawling, snow-cautious car.

At the slush-end of a hundred-yard slide,
whooping down a midnight side-street, the shock
didn't stop your laughter – not then.

Like the quick shot of three white suitcases
stacked empty inside Miss Golightly's door,
tidy and tiered as wedding cake,

which caught me out later; or the eye's pause
in the matinée-smack of sunlight
before the heart of it caves in.

Waxy Bembo

for Matthew

*'And the umpteen ways things can foul up
are beyond telling.'*
– Greg Delanty, 'The Composing Room'
(from *The Hellbox*)

We empty out our worn types of talk
into the hellbox of the Blue Bell,
compositors of coded jargon;

this dust jacket, that flyleaf, this font.
Cracking sharp faces of steely stouts,
chucking them one after another,

we set a table-breadth of reversed
letters, ill-quoined in quopping accord,
and invent a name for ambition.

Waxy Bembo. Short-hand not only
for the idea of our own poems
in the font with the superlative

italic ampersand, in covers
you could mark with a fingernail's ghost;
but for the words to blow the face off

a cliff, or to praise so well they glow
in the dark; for what we almost hear
in the chime of what we, drunk, discard.

Tour

for Polly, Matthew, Clare & Owen

I

Waves draft their first lines
onto sand, punctuate weed
with changeable stones.

★

A chough clears its throat —
splays the nib of its bill, makes
a mess of the sky.

★

Geese point caret-marks
at something missing between
one cloud and the next.

★

The hire-car's exhaust
scrawls unleaded script along
the pencil-stroke road.

★

Our quick pulses drum
like rain, charming earthworms up
to scribble on grass.

II

And spring snow rolls down
clean sheets through the sky's carriage;
try again. Again.

Canary in a Coalmine

Little lantern, caged flame,
the first to choke on gas
or absent oxygen.

Be warned – how it might end:
stiff and stained in the hot fist,
the breathless, weakening grip.

One bright spark with a song
that could ignite the dark;
bring the creaking roof in.

Bombing a Publisher

Imagine, for days after the sirens,
book-ash falling like fingerprint dust, soft
tonnes of poems making a slow Pompeii
of Manchester, the air guilty with it:

a grey broadcast among aerials,
interfering with satellite dishes,
sly in the creases of morning papers,

printing its unwelcome news on shirt-fronts
and carry-out cappuccino, trodden
down hall-carpets, making itself at home;

filling sewers with shampooey fervour,
filtering into the water-supply,
half-inching its way into lungs, leaking
into blood, heart, brain. Breathe out, now, and speak.

Clarinet Practice

for Tim

Reed music, thin as the note
of a grass blade between thumbs,

through a mouthpiece of crystal
which sang, *look, nothing to hide.*

In the big dormitory
dizzy with boot-room polish

and the closeness of sunlight,
I unkissed the brass mouthpiece,

watched the spit dry to nothing
and filled my lungs with your note

coming in across the lawn
from an open-windowed room;

and the one white vowel of it
stretched its neck, unfolded wings

and stamped a light *glissando*
across the surface tension

and up and off with big swoops,
keening and sleeking away,

trying out a lifting voice
that sang, more clearly more high,

*home is both a place ahead
and the place shrinking behind*

*and, more than these, the pure song,
the distance and the singing.*

Love Song

Press RECORD on the way out.
Shut the soundproof door

on the sigh of the speakers,
the microphone, shell-shocked,
the trembling strings,
the snare-springs' applause;

the breath, the vox,
the hours, the harmony,
translated to binary
trapped, winking, in its box.

Shut the door with a bang like a heart,
like a live wire coming unplugged.

Robinson's Message in a Bottle

All that crap about the sea –
you can lose patience with
its eternal whisperings,

eyeballs vexed and tired with waiting
for Venus or Ursula Andress
to step, pert-nippled, from the endless blue.

Palm trees curve like hula-girls
half a world away, beyond this prom's
row of dumb, angling lamp-posts.

See what I'm reduced to? The last wisp
of tobacco twisted in a slip of *Acts*
into an unglued Gideons' Rollie,

and this view propped open with match-sticks
until the penny of the day drops
and the eyes' shutter snaps shut.

I'll stop now.

The air conditioning's fucked
and this heat is killing me.
Please send more Chardonnay.

Robinson's Revenge

Hissing under the door, a corner ripped
from a half-empty page thirty,
its wrong-handed scrawl dodging the print:

My great grandfather did for Weldon Kees —
dumped his car on the Golden Gate,
fed his body to the Frisco fish —
and I'll know which day to check the obits
for Armitage, and that's money well spent.

And you — well, it won't be a Chelsea Smile
or concrete overcoat for you.
You'd do well to watch for a shadow
with bookstore carrier, mobile, broker;
the stiletto-swift fifty-one percent share.

And the corridor cracks with changing sheets,
the trolley rattles at each door in turn.

Fish on a Bicycle

Observe: boneshaker propped at the quayside
by a yacht to sail out of your life in,

and the couple who watch from the table
spread with fish-bones they've picked clean quietly

as a local bends a yard of silver
sideways over his bike's back wheel.

Notice the skeleton of spokes and tubes
holding the wheels at usual distance,

one anchoring in under its burden,
one pulling upwards like a buoy into air.

Consider how one kick at those pedals
might spin the world around the bike. *They* do,

till some movie star walks past, though his name
escapes them, his face glared in rings of low gold sun.

Flood

Afterwards, the locked house,
rattling with terrors
and ringing with quiet,
has rearranged itself:
recarpeted throughout
with water's baggage,
sofa caught in the arms
of its other half.

And the key, like a pill
on the tongue of the lock,
cracks our home open,
catches it out, light-struck.
And you, going in first
and crouching, head bowed,
untangling cables
to plug the phone back in.

And me, imagining
everything in its right place
but imperceptibly
adrift and ajar.

All at Sea

Let me tell you something – the way it is –
how the sea drags me out, makes me flotsam.
How the cold, the clown-sized orange float-suits
and the diesel-smell mean the river mouth
opening to breathe ocean. The ice-numb
space in the heart like a shock of old love
as a gull lopes around the endless hall
of sky, mewing for a window into
a wing-stilling dark that does not exist.

In the airborne second, crossing the wake
of a nuclear submarine, dry land
becomes a foreign country – the village
is whitewash-white, gardens washing-perfect
around the half-dozen sunlit houses.
Turning off the whale-path into the grey
between the iceberg overhang of prows,
the way ahead is *away* and the end
is somewhere in the oilfields at night,

unreachable in the black between flames
which are the essence of the sea's creatures
and the earth's creatures, sprung like a last breath;
the pillars of fire standing on water
leading the negligible traveller
in circles and circles, the sea twitching
its Charybdis mouth; every living thing
going up in smoke, darkening the dark
over an ocean full of dark machines.

End of the Pier Show

A birthday thought – myself, old,
    clumsy comic contraption
        rolling towards the pier's end,
bones and bronchi rattling
    like the frame of a winged bike
        gathering slow, hopeful speed.
So let's call it Cleethorpes Pier,
    where, on one early birthday,
        my fate felt sealed by a kiss
from every Nolan Sister.
    Young enough to walk its length
        without treading on the air
between the boards, I could see
    liver-coloured jellyfish
        spotting the water, and sand
wrinkling beneath creased shallows,
    and that may have been the year
        of my first family death.

One day I'll wish I were there –
    the front where the train stops dead –
        with my back against the rail
at the far end of the pier,
    watching the sun, round and brown
        as an arcade penny, slot
itself among dark buildings.
    Liner-high, a hundred yards
        out to sea, watching dunlin
stitch the ocean to the shore
    with machine-quick legs, as waves
        stretch and unravel their work,
ripping the white seam away
    and away and away.

Being neither here nor there
I will want to turn and face
    the spot where the drum of night
    might spin up a lemon sun,
feeling my lungs billowing
    like sails – like wings – as these limbs,
        their graceless assemblage of
clunks and lurches, launch themselves
    into their new element
        and,
            miraculously,
        fly.

Antony

twinned with Bénodet

As if the sea had gathered itself up
and plonked me on the sand like a statue,
bragging, *Look at that! What a piece of work!*
Jewelled with sun-drops, gowned in the taste of salt…

And a piece of work I was, porpoising
around the rocks and their cairn of my clothes,
breast-stroking in till pebbles scratched my chest
for the big effect at the standing up.

Yes, you should have seen my calves, carved in bronze,
all the muscles rolling like stones in slings –
and me in my best pants. Would have slayed you.
But that day was the day before we met.

And when you took your legendary step
from your car into this cliff-top village,
your hair alive in wind-hiss from the sea,
I felt the tongue turn to stone in my head,

and the name-plaques fixed as memorials
at the head and the foot of the one street,
the tide of you sorting the stone of me
to sand, ticking all time away, grain by grain.